ROCHESTER CATHEDRAL

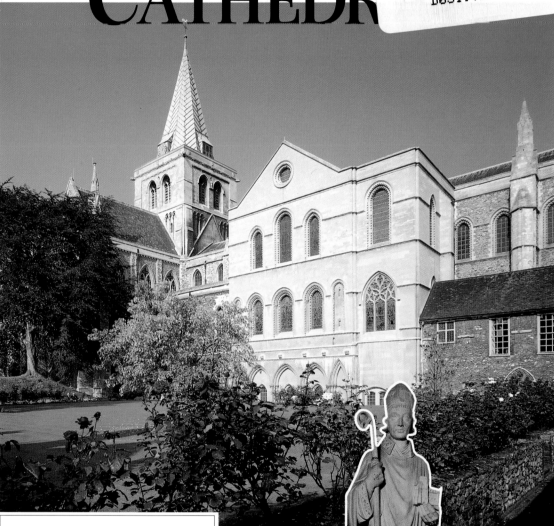

Contents

Front cover:
The view of the west front through the castle wall.

Inset: ④
The statue of Bishop Gundulf on the quire screen.

Above:
The cathedral from the south-east. The cloister was a centre of life in the Priory of St Andrew.

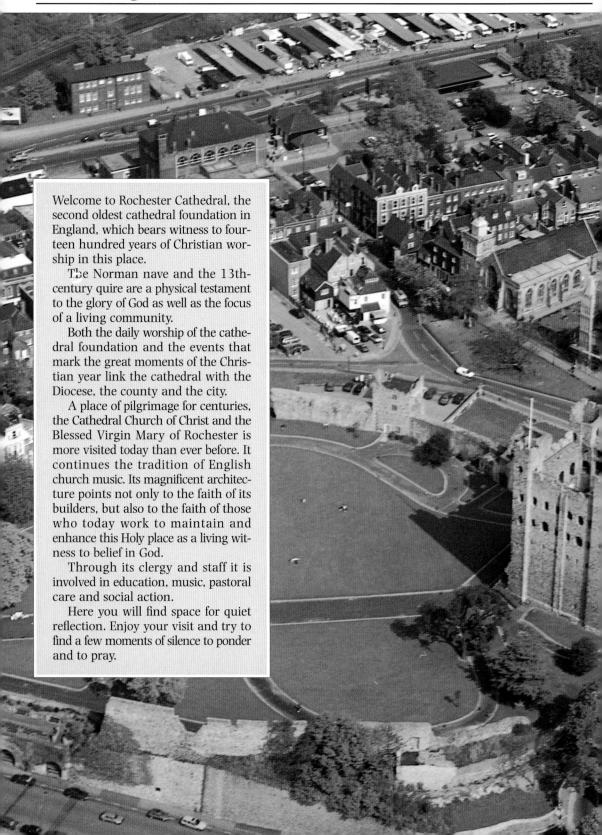

A Message from the Dean

Welcome to Rochester Cathedral, the second oldest cathedral foundation in England, which bears witness to fourteen hundred years of Christian worship in this place.

The Norman nave and the 13th-century quire are a physical testament to the glory of God as well as the focus of a living community.

Both the daily worship of the cathedral foundation and the events that mark the great moments of the Christian year link the cathedral with the Diocese, the county and the city.

A place of pilgrimage for centuries, the Cathedral Church of Christ and the Blessed Virgin Mary of Rochester is more visited today than ever before. It continues the tradition of English church music. Its magnificent architecture points not only to the faith of its builders, but also to the faith of those who today work to maintain and enhance this Holy place as a living witness to belief in God.

Through its clergy and staff it is involved in education, music, pastoral care and social action.

Here you will find space for quiet reflection. Enjoy your visit and try to find a few moments of silence to ponder and to pray.

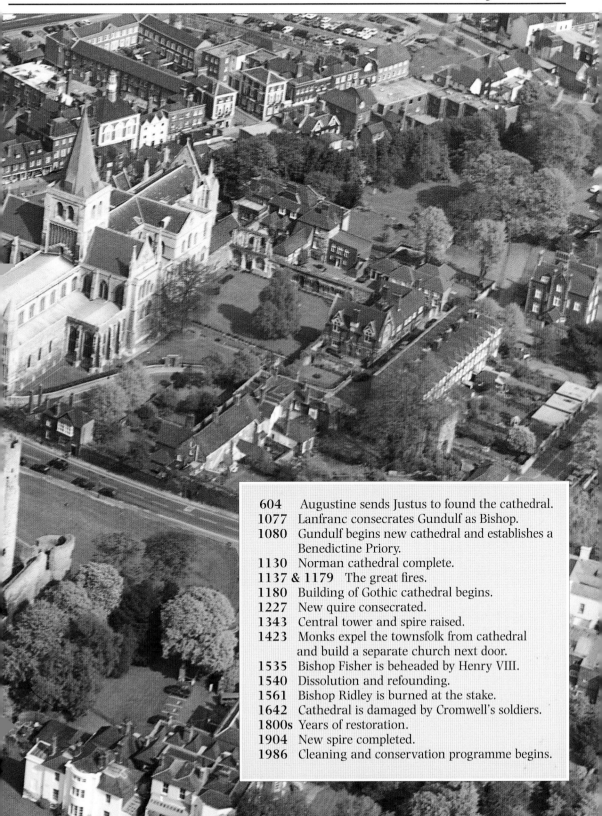

604	Augustine sends Justus to found the cathedral.
1077	Lanfranc consecrates Gundulf as Bishop.
1080	Gundulf begins new cathedral and establishes a Benedictine Priory.
1130	Norman cathedral complete.
1137 & 1179	The great fires.
1180	Building of Gothic cathedral begins.
1227	New quire consecrated.
1343	Central tower and spire raised.
1423	Monks expel the townsfolk from cathedral and build a separate church next door.
1535	Bishop Fisher is beheaded by Henry VIII.
1540	Dissolution and refounding.
1561	Bishop Ridley is burned at the stake.
1642	Cathedral is damaged by Cromwell's soldiers.
1800s	Years of restoration.
1904	New spire completed.
1986	Cleaning and conservation programme begins.

Origins of the Cathedral

Rochester's long history and culture derives from its strategic site, guarding the approach to London and the heartlands of England. Many battles have been fought here down the ages – from Ancient Britons fighting Romans to the RAF fighting the Luftwaffe. But Rochester's story is not only one of wars; it is also the story of faithfulness to the Good News of Jesus Christ, for among its great symbolic constructions are not only a bridge and a castle but also a cathedral.

The first Christians here may well have been the Roman soldiers who built a small fortified town on the site of the British settlement of Duróbrivae at the first crossing of the Medway upstream from its estuary. The foundations of the south wall of the Cloister Garth and a fragment of wall in King's Orchard to the south-east of the cathedral bear witness to the durability of Roman building materials.

Nearly 200 years after the Romans left these shores Pope Gregory sent Augustine with other monks to preach to the English nation. In AD597 Augustine was well received at Canterbury by King Ethelbert and his Christian queen, Bertha, and sought to expand his mission westwards. In 604, three years before his death, he consecrated two of his fellow missionaries as Bishops of Rochester and London. At the same time King Ethelbert built a church here dedicated to St Andrew. The diocese and cathedral are thus the second oldest in England. Although its dedication was changed at the Reformation to Christ and the Blessed Virgin Mary, the cathedral was known for many years after as the Church of St Andrew. The annual meeting of the General Chapter still takes place at St Andrewstide.

Early bishops included St Paulinus (the apostle of Northumbria and founder of the bishopric of York) whose bones lie here, and his successor Ithamar, the first man of Anglo-Saxon race to be made a bishop. He in turn consecrated the first Anglo-Saxon Archbishop of Canterbury; there is a chapel dedicated to him in the crypt.

Nothing of the original Saxon cathedral remains above ground, though archaeologists have located its foundations at the west end of the present nave.

Lying as it does close to the North Sea, Rochester suffered greatly from the attacks of the Danes. The cathedral was destroyed on more than one occasion; and there is some evidence for the existence of at least three small churches, making up a rather disjointed complex in the vicinity of the present nave.

Right: ④
The nave and the great west window seen from the quire.

Below: ②
The 19th-century font stands in an arch of the Norman nave. The style of arcade decoration is very rare, found elsewhere only in a single passageway in Canterbury.

The Norman Cathedral

By Norman standards Rochester was spiritually and economically impoverished. William the Conqueror's policy was to replace church leaders with his own men and it was to Gundulf, the second Norman monk appointed Bishop (1077–1108), that the cathedral owes its present form and magnificence. Though small in stature, Gundulf was renowned for his piety, leadership and his effectiveness as a builder (his other foundations include the Tower of London and the original Rochester Castle). He assisted Archbishop Lanfranc in establishing a Benedictine monastery here, with a complement of 22 monks which had grown to 60 by the time of his death.

Gundulf's architecture was functional, monumental and severe. Little of it remains unaltered today. He laid out the ground plan of the nave and quire, and later work was merely the reworking or enlargement of what he planned. His work is seen at its best in the nave arcading, the western part of the crypt and Gundulf's tower on the north side of the cathedral.

Wealthy and confident, the Normans embarked on a second phase of building, characterized by rich ornamentation, adventurous technical innovation and immense size. Though the smallest of their English cathedrals, Rochester is large by continental standards. The site between Watling Street and the Roman wall is constricted (for this reason the church is not properly orientated) and space had to be found for conventual buildings placed unusually to the south of the choir. Most of the Norman work in the cathedral, the remains of the cloisters and the Chapter House belongs to this period and is the work of Bishop Ernulf (1115–24) and of Bishop John of Canterbury (1125–37).

The new cathedral was consecrated in 1130 in a ceremony attended by King Henry I and no less than 13 bishops. It consisted of a nave partly for the use of the parishioners and, for the monks, a quire with aisles, rather smaller than the present one. Six bays of the original nave survive, each with differently worked piers, combining delicacy with strength. The transverse arches are possibly the earliest pointed arches in England. The nave was too broad to be vaulted in stone, but its wooden roof was destroyed in two 12th-century fires. The scorch marks may be seen on the pillars, as may medieval graffiti and traces of medieval paintings. The originally plain west façade was rebuilt c.1160 in the third phase of Norman architecture and its sculptures were finished about 15 years later, as the Gothic style was reaching England. Despite the addition of Gothic battlements and the insertion of a large Perpendicular window, this is still the finest Romanesque façade in England, its width balanced by the many small arcades and by the vertical lines of the four turrets. The south turret is wholly original. The other three were partially reconstructed from early drawings in 1889. Deep round-headed arches accentuate the majesty of the composition. The workmanship is of the very highest quality.

The Gothic Cathedral

At the end of the 12th century work began to enlarge the quire. This was a time when pilgrimages were becoming a chief feature of popular religion. The cathedral thus became a centre for pilgrimage, as well as serving parish, priory and diocese. Fulfilling these four roles remains the *raison d'être* of the cathedral today.

In 1201 William, a pious baker from Perth, stayed at the priory while on pilgrimage to the Holy Land. He was tragically murdered nearby and his body brought back to the cathedral. Miracles were reported at his tomb and before long a cult had started which brought much wealth to the priory. To the east of Gundulf's quire was added a fine square-ended presbytery (uniquely without aisles or ambulatory) and the broad quire transepts. William's tomb was placed against the north wall of the north transept. Next a shrine, destroyed with all the other shrines in England in 1547, was erected in the centre of the north transept. The walls of the Norman quire were simply encased in a solid Gothic arcade with splendid acoustic properties. The quire, which was completed in 1227, has a perfect Early English vault.

Work continued westwards along the nave. The first two bays were wholly rebuilt with Gothic arches of the same width as the Norman arches they were displacing, but high enough to take in the triforium as well. When funds ran out the work ceased at the third bay, the north side having already been dismantled and then rather clumsily re-erected. Many believe that the best early Gothic work in the cathedral is the north nave transept (*c.*1240–1255). The south nave transept was finished around 1280, its thin wooden vault designed to look like stone.

The 13th century, however, was not a time of peaceful and continuous development. The cathedral was ruthlessly plundered in 1215 when King John held it against the barons in the castle. In 1264 it was even more thoroughly desecrated by the troops of Simon de Montfort when they captured the city. The fires of the 12th century, the ravages of iconoclasts (image-breakers) at the Reformation and during the Civil War and the Commonwealth, in addition to the war damage in the 20th century, help to explain why the cathedral has a 'face that looks lived in'. Its story is

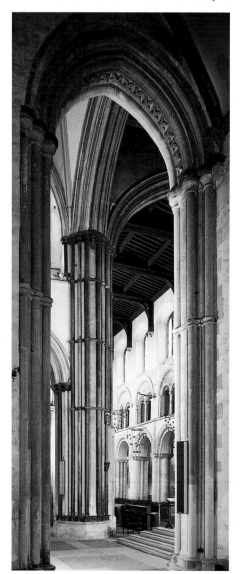

Far right: ⑦
The chapter room doorway, built as an entrance for monks attending the night offices. The main figures are Ecclesia and Synagoga (church and synagogue), both decapitated by Cromwell's puritans, but subsequently restored.

Left:
The Norman nave seen through the soaring Gothic arches of the crossing.

Below:
The alabaster effigy in the north quire transept on the tomb of Bishop Walter de Merton, Chancellor of England and founder of Merton College, Oxford. The tomb was much damaged at the Reformation, but repaired, full of anachronisms, in 1598.

the story of the English church and nation from the beginnings to the present day.

Vestiges of the Decorated period are few but important. In 1343 Bishop Hamo de Hythe raised the central tower in an antiquated style, capping it with a short wooden spire covered in lead and strengthening the supporting piers. Beside the high altar he built the sedilia – seats for the officiating clergy. Hamo's greatest gift, however, was the chapter room doorway, built as a night entrance for the monks. The intricacy and delicacy, especially of the undercutting, is the summit of the stone carver's art. The early 19th-century door is of oak, but close inspection reveals that the decoration is of cast lead.

The 15th century brought one major alteration and one major addition to the cathedral. A great window (c.1470) was set in the west wall of the nave and new clerestory windows replaced smaller Norman originals. The Norman clerestory passage was destroyed but resulted in an airy, well-lit nave which retains its Romanesque strength and character.

Last of all a Lady Chapel was added. Because of monastic buildings at the east

Left: ⑤
Thc Whccl of Fortunc, a fragment of a 13th-century wall painting in the quire. Recent cleaning has revealed the original colours, not seen for 500 years.

end, it stood at the angle of the nave and the south transept, incorporating the transept itself. The present screen has been turned through 90 degrees to bring the transept back into the main body of the church. The completion of the Lady Chapel in 1492 brought the cathedral's construction to a close.

Two Rochester Martyrs

Fisher Epilc. Roff. Præs Coll.Regin. ann. J505 cefsit ann J50

John Fisher and Nicholas Ridley, both Bishops of Rochester early in the 16th century, were men with strongly held but different religious views. Fisher was a committed Catholic, and Ridley an early English Protestant. Almost inevitably the careers and ultimately the deaths of both men were bound up in the Reformation of Henry VIII. This saw the initial moves of the English Church away from Rome towards an Anglican tradition that was gradually established later in the century by Elizabeth I.

John Fisher became Bishop of Rochester in 1504. He was a trusted councillor of Henry VII and Henry VIII, and was well known on the international scene as a close friend of Erasmus and Thomas More. However, he fell out with Henry VIII when he refused to sanction the divorce from Catherine of Aragon and the subsequent break with Rome. He would not consent to recognize Henry as supreme head of the English church. In 1535, he was accused of playing a leading part in a fabricated plot which involved Elizabeth Barton, the 'Nun of Kent', and imprisoned. In May the Pope appointed him a cardinal, which did little to help his survival, and he was executed in June. This execution was followed by that of More. It was an extraordinary occurrence, as it was the first time in English history that a bishop was executed by the monarch. Fisher's death, largely caused by the ego and paranoia of Henry VIII, resulted in widespread international protest.

Fisher had been Chancellor of Cambridge University, and during his chancellorship a group of young Protestants used to meet in the White Horse, a tavern in the city. Members of the group included two

Above left:
John Fisher, Bishop of Rochester 1504–35, and friend of Sir Thomas More. Like More he opposed Henry VIII's divorce and in 1535 was tried on a charge of denying the royal supremacy and beheaded.

Above right:
Nicholas Ridley, Bishop of Rochester 1547–50 and, after, Bishop of London. He took an active part in the Reformation, and supported Lady Jane Grey's claim to the throne. After the accession of the Roman Catholic Mary I, he was arrested and burned at the stake as a heretic.

Below:
Bishop Nicholas Ridley is burned at the stake for heresy, with Hugh Latimer, Bishop of Worcester, after refusing to acknowledge Roman doctrines in debate at Oxford.

future archbishops – Cranmer and Parker – and two future bishops – Latimer and Ridley. The latter was appointed Bishop of Rochester in 1547 and served the Protestant regime of Edward VI. However, the accession of Queen Mary in 1554 saw Ridley face demands of faith which he could not in conscience accept. He was burnt in Oxford with Latimer in that year, as was Cranmer a year later.

Fisher and Ridley both perished for their beliefs as the tides of official religious observance shifted, and their deaths characterize a somewhat tragic, if formative, period for the Christian Church in England. In the ecumenical perspective of today we give equal honour to those learned and brave men.

After the death of Mary in 1558, and the return of Protestantism under Elizabeth, Ridley's martyrdom was celebrated, and a monument stands in St Giles', Oxford, in commemoration of the three bishops who were burnt there. Fisher was not immediately remembered, but was gradually rehabilitated. He was canonized by the Roman Catholic Church in 1935 along with Thomas More.

In Rochester Nicholas Ridley is commemorated on a memorial tablet on the wall of the Baptist Church in Crow Lane, and Fisher by a memorial tablet on the garden wall of College Green, immediately south of the cathedral. The building behind that wall, now private houses, is all that remains of the palace they both occupied.

The monasteries were dissolved by 1540 but the priory was quickly refounded as a cathedral, with a Dean instead of a Prior and with no monks. The last Prior became the first Dean. King Henry VIII, however, appropriated the priory buildings as a royal palace. Hardly any trace remains of these.

The cathedral was badly damaged in the Civil War. In 1642 it was reported that 'the cathedral suffered much from the fury of the rebel soldiers under Col Sandys who, having plundered it and broken into pieces what they could, made use of it as a tippling house. The body of the church was used as a carpenter's shop and yard, several saw pits being dug and frames for houses made by the city joiners in it.' Rebuilding and repair of the fabric was a slow process after the restoration of Charles II. The King received a great welcome in Rochester on his return journey to London in 1660.

The 18th century saw a burst of building in the cathedral precinct. Minor Canon Row, for the six minor canons of the cathedral, was built then as was Oriel House and the Archdeaconry. A seventh house, for the cathedral organist, was added to the Row later.

Around this time, subsidence started to affect the south quire transept. The extent of this can be seen from the angle of the Purbeck marble pillars west of the chapter room door. The door jambs are vertical! The ugly brick infilling of a number of arches in the crypt was also carried out during this period.

This work did not suffice and L.N. Cottingham had much to do in his successful attempts (1825–40) to halt the outward tilt of the quire. He rebuilt the ashlar facing of the south quire transept and constructed the large single flying buttress on the outside of the south door. He also removed the original spire which was by then in a very poor state.

In 1840 the quire pulpit was removed and a significant portion of a magnificent 13th-century wall painting of a Wheel of Fortune was uncovered.

From 1871 to 1877, Sir George Gilbert Scott restored the roofs of the nave transepts to their medieval pitch and designed the organ case, built in two turrets placed upon the screen. His design for the high altar was less successful but he did at least do away with an inappropriate Late Gothic east window and replace it with a row of creditable 'Early English' lancets. He also floored the eastern end with encaustic tiles similar to the medieval ones in the transepts. (The oldest areas of tiled flooring still in situ in the land are to be found there.) Later in the century the west side of the organ screen was remodelled as a memorial to Dean Scott (1870 –77). The spire was replaced in 1904, but for a period of nearly 70 years after that the fabric of the cathedral may be said to have slumbered gently.

In and Around the Cathedral

Left and right:
Painted details from the walls of the quire. The pattern of leopards and *fleur-de-lis* was largely repainted in the late 19th century although a significant amount of the original 14th-century design remains immediately above the rear row of stalls on either side.

Above left:
The monument to Dean Hole (1887–1904) in the south transept.

Left: ⑥
Christ at Emmaeus – graffiti in the crypt.

Right: ⑥
The crypt, the oldest part of the present cathedral. Its main part, corresponding to the quire transept, is set out in seven aisles which originally housed seven chapels. The normal narrowing of the aisle through perspective is negated by a clever widening from the centre in the ratio of 2:3:4. There is much interesting medieval paintwork and graffiti to be seen here.

Above:
The cloister garth, or garden. In the background is the façade of the ruined Chapter House which fell into decay after being unroofed at the Dissolution. On 8 April 1540, the priory became the last monastic house to surrender to the Royal Commissioners. In the foreground is the statue of Mary and the Christ Child (1980) by John Doubleday. It was commissioned to celebrate the 850th anniversary of the cathedral's consecration.

Right:
The elegant Georgian houses of Minor Canon Row, part of the precinct to the south of the cathedral.

The Cathedral Today

In 1985 the Rochester 2000 Trust was formed under the impetus of Dean Arnold, with the result that, at long last, money for necessary and major cleaning and conservation work was made available. This was later assisted with grants from English Heritage. In recent years an extensive programme of renovation work has been carried out.

The spire has been reclad, the nave transepts reslated, the west front cleaned, the splendid nave crossing ceiling restored to its original colours and the east end cleaned and relit. Also a number of small side chapels have been removed to give greater coherence to the whole building. Completing the programme will be a major renovation of the magnificent crypt, which suffered badly in the 18th and 19th centuries from having no windows and being used as a city storehouse for over 100 years.

Built to the glory of God and proclaiming the message of Christ, this building has been a hive of activity for nearly a thousand years. As the name of the Rochester 2000 Trust indicates, the restoration work of the last decades of this century is to enable the cathedral to continue serving both city and diocese of Rochester into the next millennium.

For it is not a museum: it is not a time capsule. Rather it is a constantly changing and developing House of God with many rooms. If you stand at the nave platform and look around, you will be able to see examples of craftsmanship of every century, from Gundulf's earliest work in the nave to the 20th-century tapestries in the 15th-century Lady Chapel. Above is the splendid 19th-century nave crossing ceiling, which was superbly restored by local craftsmen in the early 1990s.

Today the cathedral is busier than ever. Within its walls a multitude of activities, both sacred and secular, for the young and the not so young, all take their turn– often in the course of a single day – concerts and recitals, ordinations and confirmations, passion plays and prize givings, study groups and school festivals.

Everyone is made welcome, whether a tourist sheltering from the rain, a visitor with a historical bent or a pilgrim with a sacred purpose. A priest is always available for those who wish to seek help.

The fundamental role of religion in the history of this nation is brought vividly to life for nearly 18,000 schoolchildren who visit this cathedral every year in organized parties for project work.

The great Anglican tradition of fine sacred music is maintained and Evensong is sung by the cathedral choir every day during term time. The choristers are all pupils of King's School, Rochester, part of

Right above:
The choir at practice. The choristers are all pupils at King's School Rochester who, to gain selection, have to meet both the exacting musical requirements of the choir and the academic demands of the school.

Right:
The cathedral seen beyond the Old Deanery – and only 50 yards from the High Street!

Below:
Votive candles are a source of both comfort and fascination, and a sign of prayer.

Below left:
An ordination of new priests and deacons, a service which has continued from the very beginning of the Christian church.

the cathedral foundation, and have to combine the demands of their school education with the requirements of the highest standards of choral music.

Mother church of the diocese and seat of the Bishop of Rochester, the cathedral also maintains a very close relationship with the county and the city and is closely involved with local matters.

Left:
Nearly 18,000 schoolchildren visit the cathedral each year in organized parties.

Below left:
Maintenance and restoration is a constant process, costing many thousands of pounds a year. Here, skilled hands work to restore the timeless beauty of the 13th-century wall paintings in the quire.

Right:
The cathedral's beautiful flowers are arranged by a rota of volunteers.

Below:
A crowded nave seen at the beginning of a service of ordination.

As the cathedral is an integral part of the fabric and history of the nation and the community, no two days here are ever the same. But there are constants: every day of the year the morning and evening offices are said or sung; every day there is a celebration of the Eucharist, and at all times places are reserved for quiet reflection and private prayer.

Admire the architectural and artistic splendours of this building, enjoy the many activities taking place within it, but find time to stop, to be quiet for a while – as untold numbers have over the centuries. For this is a special place.